THE AUDUBON SOCIETY POCKET GUIDES

A Chanticleer Press Edition

Stephen H. Amos
Assistant Director, Fairbanks Museum and
Planetarium, St. Johnsbury, Vermont

FAMILIAR SEASHORE CREATURES

Alfred A. Knopf, New York

This is a Borzoi Book
Published by Alfred A. Knopf, Inc.

Prepared and produced by Chanticleer Press, New
York.
Typeset by Dix Type Inc., Syracuse, New York.
Printed and bound by Dai Nippon, Tokyo, Japan.

First Printing.

Library of Congress Catalog Number: 90-052501
ISBN 0-679-72982-8

Cover photograph: Purple Shore Crab by C. Allan
Morgan

Introduction
How to Use This Guide 6
Identifying Seashore Creatures 8
Finding Seashore Creatures 12

The Seashore Creatures 18

Appendices
Guide to Groups 178
Glossary 186
Index 188
Credits 191

How to Use This Guide

Seashore creatures, as defined by this guide, are marine invertebrates—organisms with no backbone. Many of these creatures can be found along both the Atlantic and Pacific coasts, in tidepools and estuaries, on beaches and on pilings. Some are only visible to those equipped with masks and snorkels. Learning to recognize different types, and to identify some of the most common species, will open a complex and beautiful world to you and help you to understand the intricate relationships of many forms of life to one another.

Coverage

This new guide covers 80 of the most common and frequently encountered species of marine invertebrates in American waters. The range includes both the Atlantic and Pacific coasts, from the Arctic to South America.

Organization

This easy-to-use guide is divided into three parts: introductory essays; illustrated accounts of the Seashore Creatures; and appendices.

Introduction

As a basic introduction, the essay "Identifying Seashore Creatures" suggests an approach to the identification of these little-known animals, including general information about size, shape, color and pattern, habitat, and range. "Finding Seashore Creatures" outlines the procedures for making trips into the field, with information about timing and equipment.

The Seashore Creatures This section contains 80 color plates, arranged by family. Each account includes a full-page, full-color identification photograph. On the facing page is the text account of the species.

The text account begins with an introductory paragraph that provides interesting lore and general knowledge about an animal or group of animals. Next comes the identification paragraph, pointing out the main physical features that are keys to identification. Following this are statements of a creature's geographical range and its usual habitat. The symbol ⊗ indicates a poisonous species.

Appendices Included here are basic descriptions of the major groups of seashore creatures included in the guide, along with line drawings of the various phyla labeled to identify various body parts. Knowing family traits will help you to recognize many related species. A Glossary defines terms that may be unfamiliar to you.

Identifying Seashore Creatures

This guide is designed to introduce you to the creatures of North America's coastal waters. The introduction is, of necessity, a very basic and selective one—for there are literally thousands of species of invertebrates, belonging to dozens of groups, that could be discussed here. Familiar creatures, such as certain kinds of starfish and jellyfish, are covered in this guide, but also included are some less well-known, but still common, groups, such as the hydroids and sponges. With so many to select from, it is possible to describe only one or two species to introduce the reader to a group of organisms that may total in the hundreds. Companion volumes on marine mammals and birds will introduce you to some of the vertebrate seashore creatures.

In some cases, the seashore creatures belonging to a single genus, family, or order are very similar and can be described together in a single account. The sea fans of the genus *Gorgonia*, for example, are discussed together. In other cases, one animal may have several similar relatives in different areas; in such cases the pictured species will be the "featured" species of the account, but the others are mentioned in the text.

Size   It is frequently difficult to generalize about the size of seashore creatures—some squids, for example, are only a few inches long, while their close relatives grow to many feet. Some creatures continue to grow throughout their lifetimes, changing not only their size but also their shape (much as a caterpillar changes to a butterfly). You may find a younger specimen, and be confused because the size given in the text account refers to an older or fully adult one. Keep an open mind about sizes. Those provided here will help you distinguish between certain similar species.

Shape   Many of the groups of seashore creatures described in this guide can be recognized, in a general way, by their peculiar shape. It is easy to tell a starfish from a sea slug, for example, or a jellyfish from a sea urchin. This basic categorization of the creature is the first step in the identification process, but note that the creatures sometimes have intermediate stages quite different in both shape and habit from adults. Reading the "Guide to Groups" appendix, or leafing through the entries before going into the field, will give you basic information on the life history of the creatures covered in this guide—which are those you are most likely to discover.

9

Color and Pattern   An impressive range of eye-catching colors will greet
                     you when you look into seashore tidepools or swim in
                     shallow coastal waters. Coloration can play an
                     important role in making initial identifications,
                     especially when you are picking out individuals from a
                     mass of creatures that are frequently found together.
                     Some species may have several color forms, and so you
                     may need to review the species entry or group
                     description to make an accurate identification.

Habitat   The location in which a seashore creature is found can
                     often help in identifying it. This guide covers species of
                     seashore creatures living in a wide variety of habitats.
                     The physical condition of the shoreline, the depth of the
                     water, wide latitudinal differences in water
                     temperature, and even salinity (estuaries or bays are
                     usually less salty than oceans) should be taken into
                     account, since all these factors play a role in the location
                     of particular creatures. Using the habitat descriptions
                     in each entry will make your identification easier.

Range   Use the range information listed in each entry to
                     narrow down possibilities of what a creature may be.
                     Obviously, a sea anemone that is listed with only a

Pacific Coast range will not be found if you are on the Atlantic. But read the entry to see if the featured species has a relative or look-alike in your range. A number of species have been included in this guide because they commonly occur in both Atlantic and Pacific Coast waters.

Finding Seashore Creatures

Finding seashore creatures is easy! But determining what you have found can be much harder. In nearly every coastal marine habitat you will come across a wide sampling of seashore creatures. Of particular interest are the tidepools of the northern rocky coastlines, where anemones, starfish, and urchins abound. If you are walking along the beach, turn over small rocks (beware of sharp-edged barnacles!) to see what is under them, and keep an eye out for crab burrows, holes left by clams that have withdrawn beneath the sand, and worm tubes extending above the sand's surface. If you are studying a tidepool, search for the tentacles of tube-dwellers and burrowers, and sort through the seaweed. Other haunts of marine invertebrates are pilings and jetties, seaweed or kelp beds, shallow waters off sandy beaches, and shallow estuarine waters. Coral reefs, which contain an incredible diversity of life forms, are only touched upon in this guide, because most reefs occur outside of North American waters. Whatever shoreline you visit, you will have ample opportunity to discover a wide array of fascinating seashore creatures.

Before you explore any kind of coastline, look through this guide and familiarize yourself with the types of creatures that typically occur in the particular habitat you are visiting. Understanding the habitats will help you know what to look for and bring you satisfaction when you find the creatures you expect.

The timing of visits to certain coastlines is critically important in determining what you may find. Many sea creatures must remain in the water at all times, and so are found only from the low-tide line and below. Visiting an area at high tide may therefore prove disappointing. (Check local newspapers for the tide schedule.)

A number of marine creatures are more active at night than during the day, or in calm rather than rough seas. The existing environmental conditions will always play an important role in what you can observe on any visit to the seashore.

Of utmost importance for any shoreline observation is the right equipment. Shoes with good traction that you don't mind getting wet are essential. Around rocky shorelines, thin films of slippery seaweed or razor-sharp barnacles may cover rocks, and walking in bare feet is both treacherous and painful. If you don't want to get completely wet, a mask will allow you to glimpse the underwater world in such places as tidepools, or in shallow-water areas that allow wading.

To get a realistic idea of the variety and complexity of seashore life, however, you must be willing to go into the water. Colder water requires more equipment and precautions, but in general, all you need—other than a swimsuit—are a mask, snorkel, and flippers. Sneakers might be a better alternative to flippers if you won't be going into deep waters. Plastic bags, buckets, jars, a net, and a magnifying lens will be useful for temporarily collecting specimens to get a closer look, but remember that many seashore creatures are quite delicate and will not live for more than a very short period without the oxygen, food, or temperatures peculiar to their spot in the ocean. Be conscious of how the individual creature lives. Prying off anemones or hydroids attached to rocks may injure them, and continued walking in some areas will permanently damage the delicate life there.

The North American shores are teeming with life—with creatures large and small that cling to wave-dashed rocks or skulk about in deeper waters. Getting to know these fascinating animals will make your next visit to the seashore an exciting one, and will help you to appreciate the complex, fragile, and many-faceted relationships among all the organisms that make up our marine ecosystem. Remember, when you visit, that the diverse world of the littoral is also a delicate one. If you approach it in a respectful and responsible manner, your rewards will be boundless.

THE SEASHORE CREATURES

Finger Sponge *Haliclona oculata*

Sponges are the simplest of the many-celled animals, but even so they can be quite variable in shape. Some sponges are encrustations, others are branching, vase, or cuplike structures. The skeleton of the Finger Sponge is frequently washed up on shore after breaking free during storms. This species is also known as the Eyed Sponge because its many pores resemble eyes.

Identification   More than 18″ high. Erect, branched shape. Attached to rocks by short, narrow stalk. Tan to gray-brown or red-orange. Conspicuous pores or "eyes" scattered over the surface.

Range   Labrador to North Carolina.

Habitat   Attached to rocks in water, from the low-tide line up to 400′.

Purple Sponge *Haliclona permollis*

This is one of the more than 2,000 species of the most common group of sponges, the "horny sponges," which are named for the hard, calcareous (limy) skeleton produced by many species. Horny sponges are common on both coastlines. On the West Coast, the Purple Sponge occurs higher up on rock faces than any other species of sponge.

Identification   36″ wide. Encrusting; each raised, volcanolike area has a pore. Pink to lavender to purple. Smooth surface.

Range   Washington to central California; New Brunswick to lower Chesapeake Bay.

Habitat   Encrusted on rocks in shallow, protected areas. Also found in tidepools and on floating docks. Midtidal zone up to water 20′.

Red Beard Sponge *Microciona prolifera*

Sponges consist of a mass of individual cells, each with its own specific function. In experiments, the Red Beard Sponge has reconstructed its shape after the cells have been separated from one another. It can endure slightly polluted waters, but is most commonly found in areas with low salinity.

Identification   Thin, encrusting layer, 8″ wide. Numerous fanlike branches. Ranges from orange to red.

Range   Nova Scotia to Florida and Texas; Washington to central California.

Habitat   On rocks and pilings, various sedentary mollusks, or other hard objects in protected estuaries and bays. Found below low-tide line.

Boring Sponge *Cliona celata*

Boring Sponges start life as larvae that float in the water and settle onto shells and coral. There, they develop into small sponges and secrete sulfuric acid. The acid gradually breaks the host into small particles. In time, the sponge may completely engulf the host. In this manner, the Boring Sponge makes a contribution to the formation of sandy coastal beaches.

Identification	Individual sponges ⅛″ wide in clusters. Ivory-colored pores extend from holes in mollusks or coral.
Range	Washington to California; Gulf of St. Lawrence to Gulf of Mexico.
Habitat	On or in both living and dead mollusks and corals.

Feathered Hydroid *Pennaria tiarella*

Hydroids, relatives of sea anemones and jellyfish, occur only in brackish or saltwater areas. The Feathered Hydroid, named for its similarity in appearance to a feather, can deliver a mild sting if touched. During its life cycle, it changes from an asexual sedentary polyp to a free-swimming medusoid (jellyfishlike) form, with both male and female.

Identification Polyp colony 6″ high. Bushy and branched like a feather. Stems covered with hard, yellow to black sheath. White to pink flask-shaped head with 5 irregular whorls of knobbed tentacles below the mouth, basal whorl of 12 threadlike tentacles, and a few white to reddish-pink reproductive organs above the basal tentacles. Deep pink, cup-shaped medusa is ⅙″ high, with 4 pink-spotted radial canals and 4 short, white, bulblike tentacles around rim.

Range Maine to Florida and Texas; West Indies.

Habitat Shallow water below low-tide line, attached to solid objects. Medusa floats near water surface.

Wine-glass Hydroids *Campanularia* spp.

Hydroids frequently compose a considerable part of the marine growth on rocks, pilings, and shells in shallow water. Wine-glass hydroids are characterized by a stalked, goblet-shaped sheath that protects their feeding head. The head of these animals is bioluminescent; the light is produced by a chemical reaction.

Identification | Colony of whitish polyps, 10″ high. Fused or single, branched or unbranched, sheathed upright stems, arising from spreading base. Wine-glass-shaped feeding head. Single whorl of 20 threadlike tentacles on polyp. No medusa stage.

Range | Labrador to Florida; Alaska to S. California; Bermuda; Bahamas; West Indies to Venezuela.

Habitat | On rocks, pilings, and other hard objects, and on seaweeds. From low-tide line to water 1380′.

Portuguese Man-of-war *Physalia physalis* ⊗

Swimmers and beach-goers, beware these highly toxic animals! The stinging cells in the 3- to 6-foot tentacles of the Portuguese Man-of-war contain one of the strongest poisons known in marine animals, and they can inflict severe burns and blisters. Even dead animals can produce serious injuries. The Portuguese Man-of-war uses its inflated float, which can change shape to catch the wind, to travel the oceans.

Identification   Gas-filled float 12″ long. Iridescent pink to light blue, with a large ridged crest above and 3 types of polyps suspended beneath. Tentacles containing blue, beadlike stinging cells from 3–6′ long. Tubular feeding parts blue; mature branching reproductive organs are pink.

Range   Florida to Texas and Mexico; Bahamas; West Indies. Sometimes washed ashore after storms from Cape Cod to the Gulf Stream.

Habitat   Surface of the sea.

Sea Nettle *Chrysaora quinquecirrha* ⊗

This beautiful but mildly toxic Atlantic jellyfish produces an itchy irritation when touched; a severe sting can result in a trip to the hospital. A related species, the Lined Sea Nettle *(C. melanaster)*, can often be found washed ashore from Alaska to southern California.

Identification   10″ wide. Pink with radiating red stripes and 40 tentacles. Small, wartlike bumps on bell; shallowly lobed margin. Long, ivory tentacles alternate with sense organs along lobes. Feeding tube extends well below the bell in the form of 4 lengthy, ruffled lips.

Range   Cape Cod to Florida and Texas. Abundant in the Chesapeake Bay.

Habitat   Floats near water surface.

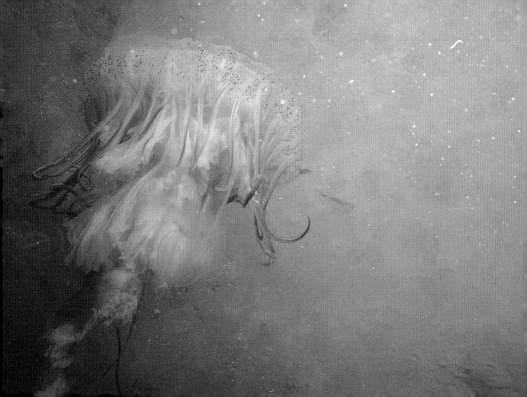

Lion's Mane *Cyanea capillata* ⊗

The world's largest jellyfish, measuring at times more than eight feet in diameter, is highly toxic. Touching the tentacles can result in severe burns and blisters, while prolonged exposure can create muscle cramps and difficulties in breathing. The Lion's Mane swims by opening and closing its bell, trailing 30- to 60-foot tentacles behind.

Identification   96″ wide. Saucer-shaped bell with smooth upper surface. Color changes with age; small specimens generally are pink and ivory, medium-sized specimens reddish to yellow-brown, and larger ones are usually a darker red-brown. More than 150 tentacles. Mouth opening has 4 folded lips forming stout feeding tube. The ribbonlike reproductive organs are suspended below the bell.

Range   Arctic to Florida and Mexico; Alaska to S. California.

Habitat   Floats near water surface.

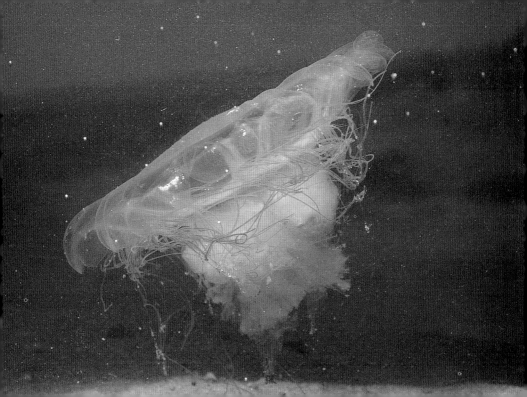

Moon Jellyfish *Aurelia aurita* ⊗

The Moon Jellyfish, the most common jellyfish, is often found up on both Atlantic and Pacific shores after a high tide or storm. It is mildly toxic, causing a sting that creates a slight rash and an itch lasting several hours. Jellyfish reproduce sexually, producing larval offspring that settle on the ocean bottom and form a hydroid colony. Hydroids, which are sedentary and asexual, simply bud off small free-swimming medusae (jellyfish), which then spread and form new colonies.

Identification 16″ wide. Saucer-shaped, translucent, white jellyfish with numerous short fringelike tentacles. Short, stout feeding tube and round or horseshoe-shaped reproductive organs tinted yellow, pink, or violet in females and yellow, tan, or rose in males.

Range Arctic to Florida and Mexico; Alaska to S. California.

Habitat Floats near the water surface just offshore.

Trumpet Stalked Jellyfish *Haliclystus salpinx*

This unusual jellyfish, also known as the Clown Jellyfish because of its festive color and shape, lives attached to plants, rocks, and other underwater objects by means of a center stalk. This extends from the trumpet-shaped body and has an adhesive pad at the tip. Smaller arms capture and move prey—mostly small shrimp—to its mouth, while small anchor tentacles assist the larger arm in moving about. Related species occur from British Columbia to northern California.

Identification 1″ high. Bright red, orange, yellow, or tan translucent body with 8 short arms ending in a burst of tentacles. Body, when flared, shows notches in between arms, where anchor tentacles are located. Mouth has 4 lips; reproductive organs located along arms.

Range New Brunswick to Cape Cod.

Habitat Attached to eelgrass, kelp, other seaweeds, and occasionally rocks. Found near low-tide line and in shallow water.

Red Soft Coral *Gersemia rubiformis*

The structure of colorful Red Soft Coral is created both by small, needlelike spicules embedded in the stems and by connective tissue holding the individual polyps together into a jellylike mass.

Identification   6″ high. Fleshy, red-orange body with club-shaped branches. Cluster of polyps on end of each branch; 8 featherlike tentacles on each polyp.

Range   Arctic to Gulf of Maine; Alaska to N. California.

Habitat   Attached to pilings, rocks, and other objects, below the low-tide line.

Sea Fan *Gorgonia* spp.

A relative of the soft corals and sea pens, sea fans look like undersea plants in strikingly bright colors. They are sensitive to light, opening their polyps for feeding on overcast days or at night. They are commonly found in warmer waters.

Identification 36″ high; flattened. Small fused branches covered with small pores form latticelike structure. Can vary from yellow to pinkish purple, rarely white.

Range S. Florida, Bermuda, Bahamas, and West Indies.

Habitat Attached to coral reefs or to rocks near reefs below the low-tide line.

Gurney's Sea Pen *Ptilosarcus gurneyi*

The Gurney's Sea Pen is a coral that looks like a feather. Usually found on soft ocean bottoms, sea pens when disturbed can completely withdraw into the mud by contracting and releasing water stored in specialized internal canals. Known as gorgonian or horny corals, sea pens—and their relatives the sea fans—contain a central support rod made of an organic matter called gorgonin.

Identification	18″ high. Plumelike, with 20 pairs of flat, widened side branches on stalk and rows of polyps along both edges. Stout, swollen base used to anchor the animal.
Range	British Columbia to central California.
Habitat	Anchored in soft muddy bottoms from below low-tide line to over 100′.

Frilled Anemone *Metridium senile*

Sea anemones resemble anemone flowers. Using waves of muscular contractions in their basal disks (also known as pedal disks), sea anemones can move several feet in a day. The Frilled Anemone can reproduce either sexually, by mating, or asexually, by division. Anemones may divide lengthwise or by leaving behind small fragments of tissue from the pedal disk as they move. This tissue will grow into new anemones.

Identification 18″ high. More than 1,000 tentacles in larger animals. White, cream-colored, olive, or reddish-brown body.

Range Arctic to Delaware; Alaska to S. California.

Habitat Colder waters. Attached to wharf pilings, rocks, or other solid objects in shallow water near the low-tide line and below.

Striped Anemone *Haliplanella luciae*

The Striped Anemone, which may have been introduced to American waters from Japanese oysters in the late 1800s, is now particularly common in Pacific waters. Sea anemones use small stinging cells in their tentacles, which can paralyze small fish, to catch their food. Smaller species carry minute food particles to their tentacles by moving cilia, or hairlike projections, on the surface of the body. They then use their tentacles to deposit the food in their mouths.

Identification   ¾″ high. Vertical stripes of cream, yellow, or orange on brown to olive-green body. Up to 50 long, slender tentacles in larger animals.

Range   Maine to Chesapeake Bay; Washington to S. California. Reported from Texas.

Habitat   On solid objects, including oysters; in shallow waters, estuaries, and salt marshes.

Ghost Anemone *Diadumene leucolena*

Sea anemones can contract abruptly from a cylindrical body shape to a short, stout shape, with tentacles and mouth pulled inwards and covered by the upper portion of the body. The translucent, pale color of Ghost Anemones gives this particular species its name.

Identification 1½" high. Translucent, whitish, pink, or olive color and a smooth columnar appearance; 60 slender ½"-long tentacles surround mouth.

Range Maine to North Carolina; California.

Habitat Among marine growth on pilings and rocks in shallow, protected waters such as bays.

Staghorn Coral *Acropora cervicornis*

This coral's name is derived from its distinctive shape. One of the most popular corals purchased by tourists, Staghorn Coral is being depleted in many reefs near populated areas. The interlocking framework of these corals provides shelter for many hundreds of species, including algae and other plants, marine invertebrates, and fishes.

Identification | 10' high. Unfused cylindrical branches variable in length. Yellowish or purplish brown; paler near the tips. Surface covered with small, round, protruding cups facing tip of branch.

Range | Florida Keys; Bahamas; West Indies.

Habitat | In protected areas of reefs, such as the windward side, and in water more than 10'.

Fire Coral *Millepora alcicornis* ⊗

Fire Coral, named for its highly poisonous sting, is actually more closely related to the jellyfish than to the true corals. People who touch it may receive severe burns, blisters, or rashes. Fire Corals, which secrete an external calcareous skeleton, grow into a sturdy, upright form and can become quite large, making it quite difficult to avoid brushing them while swimming.

Identification 24″ high. Upright and branching, or platelike, attached to coral rock or encrusted on the shells or skeletons of horny corals. Brown to creamy-colored animals, covered with tiny pores containing whitish-colored polyps.

Range Florida to Mexico; Bahamas; West Indies.

Habitat Coral reefs, cement pilings, and other large submerged objects.

Clubbed Finger Coral *Porites porites*

A member of the group of corals known as the true or stony corals, Clubbed Finger Coral is usually found along the outside, or back, edge of a coral reef. Stony corals are chiefly responsible for the formation of coral reefs and islands in tropical waters. Most are colonial and attached firmly to substrata. The Clubbed Finger Coral has a hard, calcareous exoskeleton that is secreted by the animal; it surrounds a polyp that resembles a miniature sea anemone.

Identification   Colony 12″ high, forming thick clumps of branches 1″ wide; swollen at their tips. Generally pale brown, yellowish brown, or purplish; branches covered with 1/16″ wide cups set closely together.

Range   Florida to Texas and Mexico; Bermuda; Bahamas; West Indies.

Habitat   Found throughout the reef, most commonly along the back edge, in shallow water areas.

Labyrinthine Brain Coral *Diploria labyrinthiformis*

Labyrinthine Brain Coral, a form of stony coral, has a wrinkled surface that looks like the human brain. At night, the polyps extend from the protective calcium carbonate skeleton to feed, using methods resembling those of the sea anemones—small tentacles capture food and move it to the mouth. Brain corals begin as a single polyp with a stony protective cup around it. As the polyp grows, the cup elongates, twists, and folds into its typical, recognizable shape.

Identification   96" high. Convex and rounded, with winding, interconnected valleys ¼" deep and ⅜" wide and thick walls between valleys. Bright orange-yellow to brownish yellow.

Range   Florida to Texas to Mexico; Bermuda, Bahamas, West Indies.

Habitat   Coral reefs in shallow water.

Sea Gooseberry *Pleurobrachia pileus*

The Sea Gooseberry is a member of a group of animals known as Comb Jellies, which are not true jellyfish. These animals are poor swimmers, and not able to sting. The long, sticky filaments on their tentacles capture a variety of food, including small crustaceans, fish eggs, larvae, and other planktonic animals. The Pacific form, called the Cats' Eyes *(P. bachei)*, ranges from Alaska to Baja California and is nearly indistinguishable from the Sea Gooseberry.

Identification 1⅛″ high; round to egg shaped. Transparent and iridescent, with 2 fringed tentacles; 8 rows of equally spaced comb plates extend length of body. Throat, stomach, and tentacle sheaths white, pink, yellow, or orange-brown.

Range Maine to Florida and Texas.

Habitat Near shore in shallow waters. Usually seen in large swarms.

Leidy's Comb Jelly *Mnemiopsis leidyi*

By night, most Comb Jellies glow in the dark, producing light by bioluminescence. In sunlight, they shine with a spectrum of jewel-like colors. Although they are poor swimmers, relying for the most part on oceanic currents, comb jellies use the beat of their comb plates to move through the water, with the mouth end foremost. Comb jellies are hermaphroditic—they have both male and female sex organs. Relatives such as the Common Northern Comb Jelly *(Bolinopsis infundibulum)* and Beroë's Comb Jelly *(Beroe cucumis)* are found in Pacific waters from Alaska to southern California.

Identification 4″ high. Oval and somewhat flattened at top. Milky-transparent and iridescent in color, with 2 large lobes at hind end of body, and 1 pair of short tentacles in sheaths between lobes. Comb plates in 8 rows, 2 extending down each lobe.

Range South of Cape Cod to the Carolinas; common in Chesapeake Bay as far north as Baltimore.

Habitat Shallow coastal waters, sometimes in brackish water.

Zebra Flatworm *Stylochus zebra*

Named for the distinctive striping on its body, the Zebra Flatworm is commonly found in whelk shells occupied by large hermit crabs. It is a commensal species, feeding on food fragments left by the hermit crab. Flatworms, like corals and sea anemones, have only a single opening through which food enters and wastes are discharged. The flatworm's digestive cavity branches into all parts of its body to distribute digested food.

Identification	1½" high; extremely thin. Oblong, with rounded head end and bluntly pointed rear end. Mouth near middle of underside. Yellowish to white, with numerous thin, dark brown cross bands. Row of eyespots around the margin. Stubby tentacles and brain area difficult to see.
Range	Cape Cod to Florida and Texas.
Habitat	In snail shells occupied by large hermit crabs.

Tapered Flatworm *Notoplana acticola*

The Tapered Flatworm, one of the most common flatworms on Pacific rocky shores, is an aggressive predator, hunting limpets and barnacles up to half its own size. Most flatworms have both male and female sex organs. Because the worm is so thin, every cell in the animal is close enough to the body surface to exchange oxygen and carbon dioxide directly with the environment. Flatworms move by rippling contractions of their body muscles, aided by beating cilia (hairlike projections). With these two movements, flatworms seem to glide across the surface.

Identification   2⅜" wide; flat and tapered oval, widest near the front end, with 25 eyespots in longitudinal bands on each side of head over brain. Gray or tan; darker spots along midlines. Branches of digestive tract visible when full of food.

Range   Entire coast of California.

Habitat   Under rocks between the high- and low-tide lines.

Red Lineus *Lineus ruber*

The Red Lineus is one of more than 650 species of elongated and flattened nemertean worms. These excellent predators are more commonly known as proboscis worms, because of their unusual but highly effective proboscises used to capture food. The proboscis can be extended until it is longer than the animal itself, and it is equipped with sticky mucus to trap prey, usually small annelid worms and crustaceans. The proboscis is then retracted to bring the prey to the worm's mouth.

Identification 8″ long. Slender and slightly flattened; head widest part of body. Dark red, brownish, or greenish; sometimes ringed with faint white lines; with 4–8 black eyespots and a longitudinal sensory groove on each side of the body.

Range Maine to Long Island Sound; Washington to central California.

Habitat In shallow water under rocks and shells, among mussels and in algae on both sandy and muddy bottoms.

Twelve-scaled Worm *Lepidonotus squamatus*

The Latin name for the Twelve-scaled Worm means "scaly back." When disturbed, this worm rolls itself into a tight, scale-covered ball for protection. Twelve-scaled worms are active crawlers, using their well-developed, paddlelike appendages—called parapodia—and a wriggling motion to move about the gravel or shell-covered ocean bottoms.

Identification 2″ long, with 12 pairs of oval scales. Grayish, tan, or mottled brown, with tan, reddish, or greenish projections on the scales. Pointed tentacles and antennae banded dark.

Range Labrador to New Jersey; Alaska to California.

Habitat Under rocks, among marine growth, on pilings, or on gravel or shell-covered bottoms from above the low-tide line to waters more than 8,000′.

Clam Worm *Nereis virens*

The Clam Worm is considered to be an omnivore, and its well-developed jaws are ideally suited for its life as a fierce predator of other worms and invertebrates. At times, it also feeds on carrion or certain algae. Laboratory experiments have shown that this worm has a keen sense of smell, easily locating small bits of food placed some distance from it.

Identification   36″ long. Thicker in the head region and tapered toward the rear, with 200 segments, 4 pairs of tentacles on head, and proboscis with pair of strong, black jaws. Body appendages are 2-lobed; upper part flattened and leaflike. Iridescent bluish, greenish, or greenish brown above with red, gold, or white spots; paler beneath. Appendages red.

Range   Maine to Virginia; entire Pacific Coast.

Habitat   On sandy, muddy, clay, or peat bottoms in protected waters and in brackish estuaries and among the roots of eelgrass. Found from near the high-tide line to water more than 500′.

Orange Fire Worm *Eurythoe complanata* ⊗

This highly poisonous annelid worm is frequently found in coral reefs and under stones in warm waters. It uses its bristles for defense; they become erect when the worm bends its body toward an antagonist. The bristles are brittle; if they are touched, they break off in the skin. The poison they release causes severe burning pain and itching, which can last for several days.

Identification 6″ long; flattened. Head has 5 short tentacles and 2 pairs of eyes; smooth oval pad extends from back of head to fourth segment. Orange-yellow, with tufts of red gills on upper surfaces of paired appendages. Numerous white bristles along the sides.

Range Florida, and throughout West Indies and Gulf of Mexico.

Habitat Under rocks and old coral heads on reefs from near the low-tide line to water up to 50′.

Ice Cream Cone Worm *Pectinaria gouldii*

The sedentary Ice Cream Cone Worm constructs a marvelous open-ended tube made up of a single layer of fine grains of sand, cemented together with thick mucus. The animal selects and stores even-sized grains until it can add another ring to the continually growing tube. These tubes are sometimes found washed ashore after storms. Two relatives, *P. californiensis* and *Cistenides brevicoma*, are found along the Pacific Coast from Alaska to Baja California.

Identification 1⅝" long, in a cone-shaped sand tube. Animal conical, with flattened head. Bears 2 pairs of long, tapered antennae; 2 pairs of bright red gills on sides; 2 sets of 15 large, golden bristles. Clusters of flattened feeding tentacles beneath, extending forward from mouth. Creamy pink mottled with red and blue.

Range Maine to Florida.

Habitat Tube buried vertically in sandy mud. Found in brackish waters, from near the low-tide line to waters 90′.

Red Terebellid Worm *Polycirrus eximius*

Although its body is full of red blood cells, the Red Terebellid Worm has no true circulatory system. Its tentacles, extended by forcing fluids through them, stretch out along the surface searching for food particles. The food sticks to these tentacles with mucus, and a ciliated (finely hairy) groove carries it back to the base of the tentacle, where it accumulates. The tentacles are then individually wiped over the upper lip and cilia carry the food into the mouth.

Identification 2¾″ long. Nearly cylindrical, tapered toward the rear; 25 segments, each with a pair of bristled appendages. Numerous tentacles on head; no gills or eyes. Blood-red.

Range Maine to North Carolina; many related species along Pacific.

Habitat On muddy bottoms, among eelgrass roots, or under rocks in muddy places. Does not live in well-defined tubes. Ranges into brackish waters, from low-tide line to water 55′.

Leafy Paddle Worm *Phyllodoce* spp.

Paddle worms are named for the leaflike paddles on the upper and lower surfaces of each body segment. Many are free-swimming, while others are found quite commonly on objects such as boat hulls and floats. Most paddle worms feed on other smaller sea creatures, particularly other species of worms, but are themselves eaten by a variety of ocean fish.

Identification   Up to 18″ long; slender. Head has 4 pairs of tentacles; heart-shaped lobe above mouth has 4 short antennae and conspicuous pair of eyes. Large, leaflike paddles on each body segment. May be white, tan, brown, green, or gray, with visible dark band extending down center of back.

Range   Found in the Atlantic from Arctic waters to Florida and Texas, and in the Pacific from Alaska to Mexico.

Habitat   Under rocks, on shells, in gravel, or in the holdfasts of various algae, from the low-tide line to 5,000′.

Giant Feather Duster *Eudistylia polymorpha*

Clusters of these colorful worms can transform a shallow tidepool into a showy underwater flower garden. Any disturbance causes the worms to retract with lightning quickness into their tubes. The gills of Giant Feather Dusters have numerous light-sensitive eyespots, and a shadow passing overhead may trigger this reaction. There are a number of similar species, including members of the genera *Myxicola*, *Potamilla*, and *Sabella*; they occur on one or both coasts and come in a range of sizes.

Identification 10″ long; living in sturdy, papery tubes. Animal cylindrical, slightly flattened and tapered, with collar at head end. Large plume of feathery gills, 2½″ across are visible when expanded. Tannish, with maroon, reddish, orange, or brown gills, generally with cross bands of lighter and darker shades.

Range Entire Pacific Coast.

Habitat Attached to pilings or rocks, or wedged into crevices on open rocky shores. From near the low-tide line to over 1,400′.

Spiral-gilled Tube Worm *Spirobranchus giganteus*

This beautiful worm, another sedentary marine annelid, resembles a flower growing on the surface of coral. Unlike the Ice Cream Cone Worm, which builds its tubes from grains of sand, the Spiral-gilled Tube Worm and other feather duster worms form a calcareous tube made from their own secretions. These tubes are then attached to rocks, shells, or algae, enabling the worms to live in otherwise fairly inhospitable locations. A similar species, the Spiny Spiral-gilled Tube Worm *(S. spinosus)*, burrows into coralline algae in southern California waters.

Identification 4″ long; in a large, hard tube with single spine on one side of opening. Bluish to tan animal with 200 segments, a prominent flared collar, and 2 sets of yellow, orange, red, pink, blue, white, or tan spiral gills, each 1″ long and conically shaped.

Range In coral reefs in Florida, Bahamas, West Indies, and Gulf of Mexico.

Habitat On dead coral or burrowed into living coral heads below the low-tide line in shallow seas.

84

Bushy-backed Sea Slug *Dendronotus frondosus*

The Bushy-backed Sea Slug is commonly found where there are large concentrations of hydroids, its primary food. Sea slugs are mollusks and are related to shelled snails. In the slug, the shell, mantle cavity, and original gills have all disappeared, and the body has become quite symmetrical. Large numbers of frilled or branched projections called cerata, which are actually digestive tubules connected to the slug's stomach, give this animal its bushy appearance.

Identification 4⅝" long; widest in middle and tapered to point at back end. Head blunt, with 6 branched projections extending forward. 2 comblike antennae. Back has 2 rows of 5–8 bushy projections. Usually grayish brown to rusty red, mottled with white spots, or pure white.

Range Arctic to New Jersey; Alaska to California.

Habitat On rocks and among seaweeds from the low-tide line to water 360'.

86

Hairy Doris *Acanthodoris pilosa*

This wide-ranging sea slug is most commonly found at the base of rockweed, a favorite home for many of the bryozoans and hydroids upon which sea slugs feed. The Hairy Doris lays its eggs in long white ribbons, attaching them to seaweeds or to the rocks where seaweed is fastened.

Identification   1¼″ long; oval and convex. Body covered with soft, slender, conical projections. Antennae comblike, nearly equal in size, and bent backwards. Ring of 7–9 plumelike gills located on back near rear. Can range from pale lemon-yellow to purplish brown.

Range   Arctic to Connecticut; Alaska to Puget Sound.

Habitat   On seaweeds with a heavy growth of bryozoans in shallow water near the low-tide line and below.

California Sea Hare *Aplysia californica*

Sea Hares are named for the long second pair of antennae on their heads—which resemble the ears of a hare—and for their crouched appearance. All sea hares are herbivorous, feeding exclusively on red, green, or brown algae. They feed by rasping off strips of plant material using their radula, a tonguelike appendage equipped with small teeth on its surface. The pigments in the food they eat affect their coloration. The Spotted Sea Hare *(A. dactylomela)* is a related Atlantic Coast species.

Identification 16″ long; plump and soft, with long, winglike flaps near top on both sides. Small, rudimentary internal shell remains. Head has 1 pair of antennae near mouth and a second pair above, farther back, with eyes in front of them. Foot extends entire length. Coloration depends upon food supply: reddish, brownish, or greenish, with mottled dark spots and lines.

Range N. California to Baja California.

Habitat In sheltered locations with few waves, in waters from the low-tide line to 60′.

90

Maned Nudibranch *Aeolidia papillosa*

This larger sea slug feeds predominantly upon sea anemones, with a preference for the Frilled Anemone. Its "mane" is made up of numerous small cerata, which cover the back and sides of the animal. The Maned Nudibranch's color can vary, depending on the type and color of sea anemone that make up its diet.

Identification   4″ long; thick and stubby. Back covered with hundreds of slender, fingerlike projections, with a bare area down midline. Squarish head with 2 pairs of antennae; rear end of body tapered to blunt point. Varies from whitish to gray to a tawny brown, with pale speckles.

Range   Arctic to Maryland; Alaska to S. California.

Habitat   On rocks, pilings, and mudflats where sea anemones occur, from the low-tide line to water 2,200′.

Atlantic Long-fin Squid *Loligo pealei*

Occurring in large schools, this fast-swimming squid is commonly used as fish bait and is an important food source for many commercially important fish, including sea bass, bluefish, and mackerel. A related Pacific species commonly known as Calamari *(L. opalescens)* is the squid usually sold in fish markets.

Identification 17″ long; cylindrical and tapered toward rear. Head has large pair of eyes, 4 pairs of arms about ½ mantle length, and 1 pair of tentacles ⅔ mantle length. A siphon under the neck, and a triangular fin ½ mantle length on each side of rear end. Usually white, with variable amounts of red, purplish, yellow, or brown speckles.

Range Bay of Fundy to the West Indies.

Habitat Ocean surface to water 300′ over the continental shelf.

Giant Pacific Octopus *Octopus dofleini*

One of the largest of all marine invertebrates, the Giant Pacific Octopus can weigh up to 600 pounds. All octopods produce a dark brownish ink, which they release in the water when disturbed to confuse possible predators. Members of this group have a large and complex brain and excellent eyesight, and laboratory experiments have shown that they have great learning capabilities. The related Common Atlantic Octopus *(O. vulgaris)* is native to the Atlantic.

Identification   Body can be up to 16′ long, including longest arm. Globe-shaped, with 4 pairs of arms 3–5 times body length. Arms have 2 alternating rows of suckers. Eyes placed high on the head. Wrinkled and folded skin varies in color, from reddish to brownish, with fine black lines.

Range   Alaska to S. California.

Habitat   Along rocky shores and in tidepools from the low-tide line to water 1,650′.

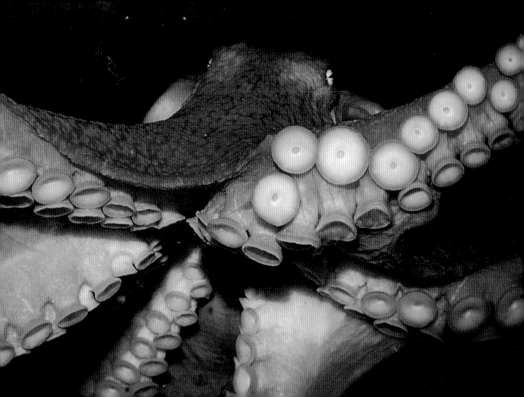

Clawed Sea Spider *Phoxichilidium femoratum*

The Clawed Sea Spider is found around rocky shores in heavy growths of tubularian hydroids, upon which it feeds. It walks on eight legs like a true spider, but it is not closely related. Sea spiders have a sucking proboscis with a mouth at the tip; some species have pinchers and feelers. The sex organs are located in the long joints of the legs, rather than in their small bodies. There are a number of both Atlantic and Pacific species.

Identification ⅛″ long; slender and flattened, with long neck and tiny abdomen. Projection behind the proboscis bears 4 eyes; 4 pairs of slender legs about ½″ long.

Range Arctic to Long Island Sound; Alaska to central California.

Habitat Along rocky shorelines in heavy growths of hydroids from the low-tide line to water up to 332′.

Common Goose Barnacle *Lepas anatifera*

The Common Goose Barnacle is primarily a creature of the open oceans, but in its larval state it favors the shaded undersides of floating objects, and therefore may be found on the bottoms of docked boats or navigational buoys. A member of the arthropod group known as crustaceans, these highly gregarious creatures are related to the true crabs, shrimps, and lobsters.

Identification   6″ long; flattened, with purplish-brown stalk up to 3″. Bears 6 pairs of extensible, feathery feeding appendages, enclosed within 5 strong, white, orange- or yellow-edged plates.

Range   Found either washed ashore or on the bottoms of floating objects along both North American coasts.

Habitat   Floating, attached to drifting objects, including buoys, bottles, or sometimes tar masses.

Giant Acorn Barnacle *Balanus nubilis*

The Giant Acorn Barnacle (*"Balanus"* means "acorn" in Latin) is the largest in a group of barnacle species, ranging in size from ¼–3½″ wide. Barnacles can be found throughout the waters of both coastlines, where they can attach themselves to any submerged object, including rocks, boat hulls, seaweeds, or other sea creatures.

Identification 4⅜″ wide; conical, white. Sides made up of 2 pairs of rough plates overlapping 1 or 2 unpaired plates.

Range Alaska to S. California.

Habitat Found on rocks, pilings, and hard-shelled animals from the low-tide line to water up to 300′.

Common Mantis Shrimp *Squilla empusa*

The Common Mantis Shrimp is well-known to shrimp trawlers as the "shrimp snapper." A quick slash of this animal's large, jackknifelike appendage can easily slice a fish or shrimp in two, or inflict serious injury to a finger. Most species live in burrows excavated in the ocean bottom, or in rock or coral crevices. They have highly developed stalked eyes, crucial for their success as predators.

Identification 10" long; shrimplike and somewhat flattened. Large front appendages have 6 sharp spines on claw; 3 pairs of walking legs; 6 heavy, marginal spines on tailpiece.

Range Cape Cod to Florida and Texas; south to Brazil.

Habitat Burrows into muddy or sandy bottoms, from low-tide line to water up to 500'.

Horseshoe Crab *Limulus polyphemus*

The Horseshoe Crab is a relative of the spider, and not a true crab at all. Mating pairs of this common seashore creature are found in large numbers along Atlantic beaches during the spring, with the males clutched onto the back of the females. The females dig holes in the sand above the low-tide line and lay 200–300 pale green eggs, which are fertilized by the male and then buried. Young horseshoe crabs, which resemble miniature adults, hatch in several weeks.

Identification   24″ long. Tannish, horseshoe-shaped carapace, triangular abdomen, and long, spiked tail. Pair of compound eyes on each side of carapace; 2 simple eyes on forepart of midline. Mouth, on underside, surrounded by 5 pairs of walking legs and a pair of pinchers.

Range   Gulf of Maine to Gulf of Mexico.

Habitat   On muddy or sandy bottoms in water ranging from the low-tide line to 75′.

106

California Beach Flea *Orchestoidea californiana*

Like fleas, Beach Fleas can leap a foot or more. At night, these creatures can be seen in tremendous numbers on sandy beaches above the water line, where they feed on organic debris, particularly seaweeds, washed up by the waves. The Big-eyed Beach Flea *(Talorchestia megalophthalma)* is a related Atlantic Coast species.

Identification   1⅛″ long; broad, arched appearance. Second pair of antennae longer than body; orange in juveniles and red in adults. Eyes black. Has 7 pairs of walking legs, the last 2 pairs bent back toward the abdomen.

Range   British Columbia to S. California.

Habitat   Wide, sandy beaches along the open shore, near the high-tide line and above.

Coon-striped Shrimp *Pandalus danae*

The Coon-striped Shrimp, when young, is a functional male, but it becomes a fertile female when it matures. This genus is one of several groups of commercially fished shrimps in American waters. The Maine Shrimp *(P. borealis)* is a common species in northern Atlantic waters.

Identification 5¾" long. Irregular blue stripes and occasional white spots on body.

Range Alaska to central California.

Habitat Bays, estuaries, and eelgrass beds, but also in tidepools, from the low-tide line to waters over 600'.

Pink Shrimp *Penaeus duorarum*

The Pink Shrimp, along with similar species, the Brown Shrimp *(P. aztecus)* and the White Shrimp *(P. setiferus)* make up a high percentage of the commercial shrimp catch in Atlantic waters. These shrimp generally live on sandy ocean bottoms, in waters 15–100 feet deep. Shrimp boats pull V-shaped nets, which trap the bottom-dwelling shrimp in the apex of the bag formed by the arms of the net.

Identification Males 6½" long; females average 1" longer. Both sexes somewhat flattened. First 3 pairs of walking legs have pincers for capturing and holding food.

Range Chesapeake Bay to Florida and Texas; Bermuda; Bahamas; West Indies to Brazil.

Habitat On various substrates of ocean bottoms, from the low-tide line to waters up to 300'.

Red-lined Cleaning Shrimp *Lysmata wurdemanni*

Cleaning shrimps, named for their interesting associations with a variety of sea creatures, remove parasites and diseased tissue from the skin and pick bits of food from between the teeth of many different kinds of fishes. Cleaning shrimps remove silt and organic debris from sea anemones and corals and—with their bright colors—act as lures for hungry fish, which are then nabbed by the anemone. Although most cleaning shrimps occur in warm waters, those of the genus *Lysmata* can readily be found in waters up to the Chesapeake Bay or to central California.

Identification 2¾" long; tapered toward rear end. Translucent white, with longitudinal red stripes down back and transverse stripes on sides.

Range Chesapeake Bay to Florida and Texas; Bahamas; West Indies to Brazil.

Habitat On rocks, jetties, and coral reefs among hydroids, near the low-tide line to water 100'.

Northern Lobster *Homarus americanus*

This large and tasty crustacean is an important catch for Atlantic Coast fishermen. Weighing up to 48 pounds, the Northern Lobster has two very different pincers—one used as a crusher to open hard objects, such as snails or clams, and the other a cutter for tearing apart prey, carrion, or vegetation. The Northern Lobster lives in inshore waters during the summer months, moving to deeper water during the winter.

Identification   34″ long; large, dissimilar pincers and cylindrical carapace. First of 2 sets of antennae longer than body. First 3 pairs of walking legs have pincers; first pair greatly enlarged. Varies from greenish black to yellow or blue above, paler underneath; appendages tipped in red.

Range   Labrador to Virginia.

Habitat   On rocky bottoms both in bays and in open ocean waters, from near the shoreline to the continental shelf.

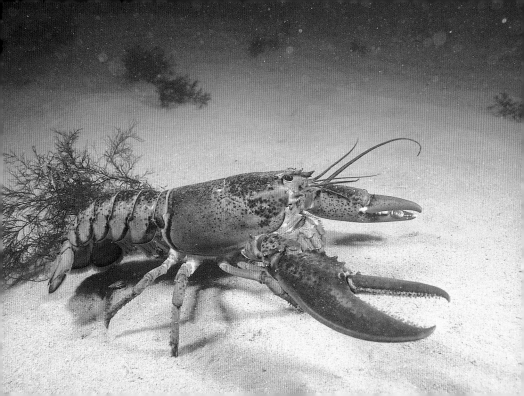

Ridged Slipper Lobster *Scyllarides nodifer*

Also known as the Spanish Lobster, the Ridged Slipper Lobster has antennae that have evolved into flattened, spadelike tools used to shovel and push the ocean bottom as the lobster looks for food. The animal's greatly flattened carapace allows it to slip comfortably into its favorite home—narrow crevices in coral reefs.

Identification	12″ long. Broad, flattened carapace covered with bumps. Strong second pair of antennae used as shovels for digging. No differentiation in walking legs, as with other lobster genera.
Range	S. Florida; Bahamas; and West Indies.
Habitat	In or around coral reefs and the sandy bottoms that surround them, in shallow to moderately deep waters.

California Rock Lobster *Panulirus interruptus*

Although this creature lacks the greatly enlarged pincers of the Northern Lobster, the California Rock Lobster has numerous spines that provide great protection from predators and commercial fishermen alike. The West Indies Spiny Lobster *(P. argus)* is a close relative species found in southern Atlantic waters.

Identification   16″ long, with long, cylindrical body carapace. Spines cover upper body surface, as well as base of second pair of antennae, which are longer than the body. No pincers on walking legs. Usually reddish brown, with red spines and legs marked with pale brown longitudinal stripes.

Range   Central California to Baja California.

Habitat   Among rocks in tidepools, from the low-tide line to moderately deep waters.

Long-clawed Hermit Crab *Pagurus longicarpus*

The Long-clawed Hermit Crab is the most common species found in Atlantic waters. Hermit crabs inhabit snail or whelk shells, which they need to protect their soft, vulnerable abdomens. They must continually search for new, larger shells as they grow. There are a number of genera and species of hermit crabs; the Grainy Hermit Crab *(P. granosimanus)* being most common in shallow Pacific waters.

Identification ½″ long; found living in snail shells. Right pincer larger than left. Grayish or greenish white with tannish stripe on pincer.

Range Nova Scotia to Florida and Texas.

Habitat Ocean bottom, including sandy, muddy, rocky, or weedy areas; along open shores and protected estuarine waters, from the low-tide line to water 150′.

Pacific Mole Crab *Emerita analoga*

Large populations of mole crabs can often be seen on open beaches, scurrying in the shallow beach surf or digging into the wet sand. They feed by burying themselves seaward, and then using their fringed second antennae to filter plankton and detritus from receding waves. The Atlantic Mole Crab *(E. talpoida)* is a closely related species.

Identification 1⅜" long. Egg shaped with hard, convex carapace. Long and feathery second pair of antennae, usually concealed under edge of pale, grayish carapace. Tailpiece bent forward under body to conceal the rear end of the undersurface.

Range Alaska to Peru and Chile.

Habitat Open, sandy beaches between the high-tide and low-tide lines.

Blue Crab *Callinectes sapidus*

This common, delicious crab supports an extensive commercial seafood industry from the Chesapeake Bay to the Gulf Coast. Most crabs cannot swim, but this creature has flattened, paddlelike rear legs that allow it to be the fastest and most agile of all crustaceans, swimming forward, backward, or sideways.

Identification 9¼″ wide. Large spines at either end of bluish-green, spindle-shaped carapace. Large, powerful pincers, bluish on male and red on females.

Range Nova Scotia to Florida and Texas; Bermuda; West Indies to Uruguay.

Habitat In shallows and in brackish water from low-tide line to water 120′.

Red Crab *Cancer productus*

Adults of this Pacific Coast crab are uniformly red in color, although juveniles can vary from white, brown, or blue to red or orange, and be either solid or patterned. Another closely related Pacific Coast species, the Dungeness Crab (*C. magister*) is the primary commercial crab on the West Coast.

Identification 6¼" wide. Smooth, fan-shaped carapace brick-red in color. Pincers are short and bent downward at tips.

Range Alaska to S. California.

Habitat Among rocks and in tidepools along open rocky shores and in bays and estuaries, from the low-tide line to water 260'.

Purple Shore Crab *Hemigrapsus nudus*

Known as the Purple Shore Crab for its habit of spending time on rocks out of water, this Pacific Coast crab feeds primarily on algae scum growing on rocks, but it will also scavenge animal matter. The Yellow Shore Crab (*H. oregonensis*) and the Striped Shore Crab (*Pachygrapsus crassipes*) are related Pacific Coast species. The Mottled Shore Crab (*P. transversus*) ranges from North Carolina to Florida and Texas in Atlantic waters.

Identification	2¼" wide; round, purplish-black, reddish-brown, or greenish-yellow carapace. Large, equal-sized pincers in male; covered with purple or red spots.
Range	Alaska to Baja California.
Habitat	On open rocky shores among seaweeds, in protected bays and estuaries.

Purple Marsh Crab *Sesarma reticulatum*

This colorful crab lives in burrows, sheltered by mud huts, in salt marshes. It frequently shares its residence with fiddler crabs. The Purple Marsh Crab is strictly vegetarian, feeding on marsh grass, which it cuts using its sharpened pincers. Another related Atlantic species, the Wharf Crab *(S. cinereum)* is also known as the "friendly crab" for its habit of climbing into open boats.

Identification	1⅛″ wide; squarish purple, olive, or blackish carapace. Relatively large orangish pincers.
Range	Cape Cod to Florida and Texas.
Habitat	Salt marshes and mud flats, among marsh grass beds.

Ghost Crab *Ocypode quadrata*

Ghost Crabs scavenge along the beach for bits of food during evening hours. Their sandy color, which allows them nearly to disappear into their surroundings, and their swift speed give them a ghostly appearance. Their burrows—with mounds of sand from continued excavation near the entrance, and many tracks left by their sharp toes—are easily spotted above the high-tide line.

Identification   2″ wide. Rectangular body with large, club-shaped eyestalks. One large pincer; walking legs long and hairy. Grayish or yellowish-white upper surface, with white below. A touch of lavender on pincers.

Range   Rhode Island to Florida and Texas; West Indies to Brazil.

Habitat   Sandy beaches above the high-tide line.

Sand Fiddler *Uca pugilator*

Fiddler crabs are usually found along tidal creeks or in marshes. The male's extraordinary large pincer is not a weapon, but is used only in courtship displays. There are several Atlantic species of fiddler crabs, but the sole Pacific species, the California Fiddler *(U. crenulata)* has an uncertain future due to human development of its habitat.

Identification 1½" wide; rectangular carapace with long, slender eyestalks. Males have one large pincer, either left or right, nearly twice body width; females have small, equal-sized pincers. Purplish or grayish blue with irregular black, brown, or grayish markings.

Range Boston Harbor to Florida and Texas; West Indies.

Habitat On protected sand and sandy mud beaches, in marshes, and along tidal creeks.

Common Spider Crab *Libinia emarginata*

The Common Spider Crab can usually be found along the intertidal zones on various substrates, but most frequently in seaweed beds. Its carapace is often covered with solidly attached strands of algae, which grow on the sturdy surface and provide camouflage for the slow-moving animal.

Identification 4″ long. Round body and legs, with male's pincers frequently more than 6″ long; shorter in females. Spiny carapace can be grayish yellow or brown.

Range Nova Scotia to Florida and Texas.

Habitat Ocean bottom surfaces, particularly seaweed beds, from the low-tide line to water up to 410′.

Arrow Crab *Sternorhynchus seticornis*

Named for the triangular, arrowlike shape of its body, the Arrow Crab has begun to appear in pet stores and aquariums in recent years. Generally found in warmer waters, this delicate little crab is enchanting to watch as it maneuvers its way among the rocks or across a reef.

Identification   2¼″ long. Pale gray, cream, buff, or orange arrowhead-shaped carapace with inverted, V-shaped light- and dark-brown or blackish stripes. Pincers are twice body length; bright red legs are 3 times body length.

Range   North Carolina to Florida and Texas; Bermuda; Bahamas; West Indies to Brazil.

Habitat   Rock, shell, sand, and coral-rubble bottoms, coral reefs, jetties, and wharf pilings, from the low-tide line to water nearly a mile deep.

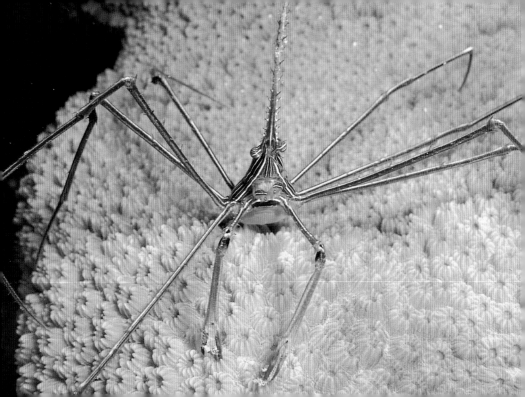

Spiny Sun Star *Crossaster papposus*

One of the most beautiful of all starfish, the Spiny Sun Star is a fierce predator that feeds almost exclusively on smaller starfish. Starfish move across the ocean floor using numerous, slender tube feet on their undersurface, which are operated by an internal hydraulic system that pumps water in and out, creating a purposeful, coordinated motion. Tube feet with suckers reach ahead and attach to an object, then pull the sun star forward.

Identification — 14″ wide; 8–14 arms, ½ length of animal. Upper surface covered with brushlike spines. Scarlet, with concentric bands of white, pink, yellow, or dark red.

Range — Arctic to Gulf of Mexico; Alaska to Puget Sound.

Habitat — On rocky bottoms from low-tide line to 1,100′.

Bat Star *Patiria miniata*

The Bat Star, clearly the most common species of starfish along the Pacific Coast, is particularly fond of kelp forests. Starfish feed themselves by wrapping their arms around their prey, attaching themselves to it with their tube feet, and then everting the forepart of their stomach to envelop the prey. The food is gradually digested.

Identification 8″ wide; 4–9 (usually 5) short, thickly webbed arms. Commonly reddish orange, but both color and pattern can be highly variable.

Range Alaska to Baja California.

Habitat On rocks, in kelp forests, and on sandy bottoms from the low-tide line to water 960′.

144

Northern Sea Star *Asterias vulgaris*

An abundant species in northern waters, this variably colored sea star preys largely upon mussels. Many types of sea stars can regenerate lost arms. When damaged, an arm is shed at a point close to the central disk, even if the damage has occurred close to the tip. Once the cut surface heals, a new arm regenerates.

Identification   16″ wide. Soft, flabby body. Long arms tapered toward the tip and somewhat flattened. Colors vary remarkably, including pink, rose, tan, cream, gray, bluish, greenish, lavender, or purple. Red eyespot is visible at each arm tip.

Range   Labrador to Cape Hatteras.

Habitat   Rocky or gravel bottoms, from the low-tide line to water 1,145′.

Northern Basket Star *Gorgonocephalus arcticus*

Basket stars are named for their long, flexible, and extensively branched arms. The suckerless tube feet on the undersurface serve as sensory organs, while the arms are used in moving and in grasping food. The creature is frequently completely entangled in whatever it has grasped; it is commonly found in lobster pots, attracted by the bait.

Identification   32″ wide; with mass of tendril-like coils. Mouth has 5 sawlike jaws in shape of star. Pentagon-shaped leathery disk is yellowish brown or darker brown.

Range   Arctic to Cape Cod.

Habitat   Rocky bottoms in water 18–4,800′.

Daisy Brittle Star *Ophiopholis aculeata*

Many species of brittle stars are found on one or both coastlines of North America. This relatively common, elegant-looking creature can generally be found in tidepools under rocks, although it quickly scurries to cover when disturbed. The Daisy Brittle Star also frequents the bases of kelp plants, sweeping its lead arms back and forth as it moves forward until it locates something edible. Brittle stars are aptly named, since their arms break off easily when handled or disturbed.

Identification	8″ wide. Orange, pink, yellow, white, blue, green, tan, gray, or black, with an infinite variety of spots, lines, bands, or mottlings.
Range	Arctic to Cape Cod; Bering Sea to S. California.
Habitat	Under rocks in tidepools and among kelp holdfasts, from the low-tide line to water over a mile deep.

Green Sea Urchin *Strongylocentrotus droebachiensis*

The Green Sea Urchin is abundant in certain protected bays. Most sea urchins are omnivorous, eating sponges, coral polyps, mussels, dead and dying animal matter, and various algae. The skeleton, which is known as the "test," is covered with protective spines. The undersurface tube feet, which reach out between the spines, are tipped with suckers used chiefly in movement. The Purple Sea Urchin *(S. purpuratus)* is a closely related species native to Pacific rocky shores.

Identification 3¼″ wide. Spines, equal in length, cover the oval-shaped test. Brownish green, with light green or grayish-green spines.

Range Arctic to New Jersey; Alaska to Puget Sound.

Habitat On rocky shores and in kelp beds, from the low-tide line to water up to 3,795′.

Long-spined Urchin *Diadema antillarum*

The Long-spined Urchin—assiduously avoided by bathers and divers in the American tropics—has spines that can easily puncture wetsuits or tennis shoes, and can produce intense irritation if lodged in the skin. Urchins eat by using a specialized toothed organ called "Aristotle's lantern"; this organ is made up of a complex system of skeletal rods and muscles, and its motion operates five teeth. These teeth methodically gnaw away at the urchin's food, and can dig depressions in reefs or on rocks for protection.

Identification Test 4″ wide; long, sharply pointed spines reach 16″. Adults dark purple or black; young may have white bands or speckles on spines.

Range Florida; Bermuda; Bahamas; West Indies; Mexico to Suriname.

Habitat Frequents coral reefs, rocks, coral rubble, reef flats, or tidepools; can be found below the low-tide line in shallow waters.

Slate-pencil Urchin *Eucidaris tribuloides*

The broad spines of Slate-pencil Urchins are frequently coated with a variety of marine growth, including sponges, coralline algae, and bryozoans. Its spines, when shed, can sometimes be found along coral sand beaches; they produce a pleasing, musical sound when strung together to make a wind chime.

Identification   Test 2½″ wide; heavy, blunt spines nearly the width of test. Red-orange to brown, with brown-spotted or striped tan spines, sometimes tinged with red or green.

Range   South Carolina to Florida; Bermuda; Bahamas; West Indies; Mexico to Brazil.

Habitat   On coral reefs and among rocks or coral rubble below the low-tide line in shallow waters.

Common Sand Dollar *Echinarachnius parma*

Sand dollars, and their close relatives the sea biscuits and heart urchins, are cousins to the true sea urchins. Like the more highly developed sea urchins, they have the specialized mouthparts known as "Aristotle's lantern." Living in sandy or muddy substrates, sand dollars feed on fine particles of organic matter and burrow through substrates using the modified tube feet on both their under and upper surfaces. The Eccentric Sand Dollar *(Dendraster excentricus)* is commonly found along the Pacific coastline.

Identification   Flat, disklike test 3⅛" wide. Usually reddish or purplish brown, paler below. Washed-up test of dead animal is snowy white.

Range   Labrador to Maryland; Alaska to Puget Sound.

Habitat   On sandy bottoms from the low-tide line to water a mile deep.

Red Sea Cucumber *Cucumaria miniata*

The Red Sea Cucumber has a curved body that fits into crevices in rocks and that allows it to expose both its tentacled mouth and hindparts to moving water. These tentacles are actually modified tube feet similar to those found on urchins, sand dollars, and sea stars. The Orange-footed Sea Cucumber *(C. frondosa)* is a large and brightly colored sea cucumber found in New England waters.

Identification 10″ long; cucumber-shaped with 10 highly branched, retractable, orange tentacles. Brick-red, although bright orange, pinkish, or purple specimens not uncommon.

Range Alaska to central California.

Habitat In crevices and under rocks below the low-tide line in shallow waters.

Hairy Sea Cucumber *Sclerodactyla briareus*

This species of sea cucumber lies partially buried in muddy or sandy bottoms. The tentacles of sea cucumbers are actually modified tube feet, and can regenerate within several weeks if shed. Sea cucumbers are elongated and lie on their sides, with rows of well-developed tube feet along the underside touching the substrate.

Identification   4¾″ long. Nearly covered with small tube feet, giving the creature a hairy appearance. Mouth surrounded by 10 bushy tentacles. Black, brown, green, or purple.

Range   Cape Cod to Florida and Texas; West Indies.

Habitat   Sandy or muddy bottoms from the low-tide line to 20′.

Spiral-tufted Bryozoan *Bugula turrita*

The Phylum Bryozoa consists of more than 4,000 species of colonial, sedentary animals. Individuals in the colonies are no more than $\frac{1}{32}''$ in size, yet the colonies may reach several feet across. The Spiral-tufted Bryozoan is one of the most spectacular of the Bryozoa. Its individual animals are arranged in two parallel rows, and the secondary branches are arranged in a spiral pattern. The California Spiral-tufted Bryozoan *(B. californica)* is a similar Pacific Coast species.

Identification	Plantlike appearance; colony 12″ long; with erect, flexible branches. Generally orange-brown or tan.
Range	Massachusetts to Florida.
Habitat	On pilings, rocks, seagrasses, or algae from low-tide line to 90′.

Sea Vase *Ciona intestinalis*

A large Sea Vase can pump more than five gallons of seawater each day through its system to obtain food, receive oxygen, and excrete waste. During larval stages, this creature has a tubular dorsal nerve cord, as well as a notochord, a stiff internal rod that provides both firmness and flexibility. Therefore, it is considered a Chordate, but one of a minority without a true skeleton.

Identification 6″ high. Slender and vaselike; pale yellow or greenish, translucent body.

Range Alaska to S. California; Arctic to Rhode Island.

Habitat On rocks, pilings, floats, and boat hulls in harbors and protected bays from the low-tide line to 1,650′.

Monterey Stalked Tunicate *Styela montereyensis*

The Monterey Stalked Tunicate is a common, easily
recognized, and broadly distributed species of solitary
tunicate. Also known as sea squirts, tunicates have
different openings, or siphons, through which they
bring in and expel water; the water carries food and
oxygen into the body, and transports waste away. The
Striped Tunicate *(S. plicata)* can be found along
southern Atlantic and Pacific coastlines.

Identification 10″ high; shaped like a long bowling pin. Yellowish to
reddish brown, thick and leathery tunic.

Range British Columbia to Baja California.

Habitat On rocks in both exposed and protected areas, from the
low-tide line to water 100′.

Sea Peach *Halyocynthia pyriformis*

Named for its shape, color, and fuzzy surface, the Sea
Peach has a tadpole-shaped larva with both a notochord
(a stiff internal rod) and dorsal nerve cord. Most
individual sea squirts have both male and female sex
organs, releasing eggs and sperm into the water for
fertilization. The free-swimming larva settles into an
appropriate location to mature, in the process losing its
chordate characteristics as well as its muscular tail.

Identification   5″ high. Resembles a ripened peach; fuzzy yellow to
orange, tinged with red at top and on one side. Rootlike
fibers at bottom attach to substrate.

Range   Arctic to Massachusetts Bay.

Habitat   On rocky or gravel bottoms from the low-tide line to
water 637′.

Common Salp *Salpa fusiformis*

Salps are free-swimming, transparent sea squirts, which sometimes can be found blown ashore by the thousands in summer and autumn. Salps reproduce both sexually and asexually, with the asexual form producing a long chain of buds that trails behind the creature when swimming. Salps move about by taking in water through the front ("incurrent") siphon, then forcibly squirting it out the other end. Two related species, the Horned Salp *(Thalia democratica)* and the Common Doliolid *(Doliolum nationalis)* also can be found along both coastlines.

Identification 3¼″ long. Colorless, transparent cylinder.

Range Alaska to California; entire Atlantic Coast.

Habitat Floats in plankton on the ocean surface.

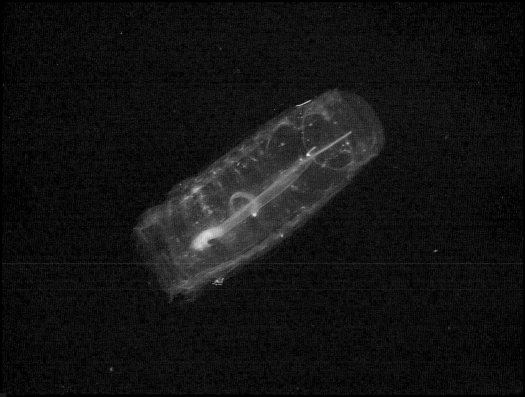

Lined Chiton *Tonicella lineata*

The shell in this unusual group of mollusks is made up of eight loosely connected plates surrounded by a girdlelike margin to the mantle. The odd configuration of these plates allows chitons great flexibility in movement, and they can easily shape themselves to whatever object they are on. If picked up, they will immediately try to roll into a ball for protection. Although most chitons are found in the Pacific, a number of forms also occur from the northern Atlantic to the tropics.

Identification 2″ long. Oval body. Distinctive colorings with zigzagging lines of red, blue, white, brown, or black on a mottled reddish-brown background. Mantle is greenish or yellowish.

Range Found from Alaska to S. California.

Habitat From the low-tide line to 180′; on rocks covered with coralline algae.

174

Giant Keyhole Limpet *Megathura crenulata*

The Giant Keyhole Limpet gets its name from the hole at the apex of its shell; through this the creature expels food- and oxygen-bearing water brought in by the mantle (the soft body). Most of the shell is concealed by the mantle, which spreads over it. A relative of the snail, this limpet feeds primarily on colonial tunicates and algae, using its rasping tongue, or radula, to scrape the food from rocks and other surfaces. Other species of keyhole limpets occur throughout the Pacific Coast and in northern Atlantic waters. The naturally pierced shells were strung on belts and used by Native Americans for ornament and as money.

Identification   Up to 5⅛" long. Oval body usually longer and wider than shell. Outer shell pinkish tan, with underside white. Mantle varies from black to gray, and foot is yellowish orange.

Range   Central California to Baja California.

Habitat   Near the low-tide line to well below, in crevices and on rocks and breakwaters.

Guide to Groups

Described here are the major groups of seashore creatures—families, classes, and phyla—that are included in this guide.

Sponges (Phylum Porifera)

Sponges are multicellular sea creatures that have no body organs or mouths. They circulate water through numerous pores and chambers within their bodies by using flagellated cells at the entrance of the cavities. Sponges are almost all sedentary, and they have an unusual skeletal system of spicules used in support.

Cnidarians (Phylum Cnidaria)

Also known as coelenterates, cnidarians have developed primary radial symmetry, and have a single mouth opening. Most have stinging tentacles encircling the mouth opening. Cnidarians have no brain, stomach, or excretory system. Certain classes have several forms, including a sedentary cylindrical polyp stage and a free-swimming medusa stage.

Hydroids (Class Hydrozoa)

Hydroids begin life as asexual polyps that divide and become medusae, or sexually reproductive jellyfishlike creatures. They have a structureless mesoglea and no stinging cells.

Jellyfish (Class Scyphozoa)

We commonly think of jellyfish as they appear in the medusa stage. They have a thick, firm mesoglea, and the mouth tube has four mouth arms surrounding it. There are stinging cells along the walls of the stomach.

Corals and Sea Anemones (Class Anthozoa)

The stomach in these creatures is separated into distinct radial chambers. The mouth is located on an oral disc, surrounded by tentacles. Sexes are usually separate. Soft corals are colonial, forming flexible structures into which the polyps can retract. Sea anemones are solitary, with strong basal muscles that attach to objects or dig into the substrate. Stony corals deposit a hard structure formed from calcium carbonate in which the polyps live colonially.

Comb Jellies (Phylum Ctenophora)

These animals are distinguished from true jellyfish by their ciliated comb plates, which are used in movement. They have a single stomach cavity and do not sting. Comb jellies are hermaphroditic; a single creature contains both male and female reproductive organs.

Flatworms (Phylum Platyhelminthes)

Flatworms have only a single body opening, the mouth, into which food is taken and through which wastes are excreted. As their name implies, they are very thin in comparison to their width and length. They have well-developed nervous, muscular, excretory, and reproductive systems that are protected within a layer of tissue—an advance over the cnidarians.

Nemertean Worms (Phylum Rhynchocoela)

These creatures can stretch to many times their relaxed body length. They have both mouth and anus, and the sexes are separate. They are highly predatory, hunting by thrusting out from their mouths a long proboscis, which secretes mucus that entangles their victims.

Segmented Worms (Phylum Annelida)

There are more than 6,000 species of marine annelid worms. Their elongated and cylindrical bodies are made up of a series of segments. The predatory types move about with well-developed, paired parapodia (or legs). The filter-feeding sedentary types have no eyes or appendages; they live in excavated tubes. Some sedentary types have feeding tentacles.

Mollusks (Phylum Mollusca)

Most mollusks produce a shell, or valve, and have a body made up of three parts—the head containing a mouth and brain, the visceral mass containing the body organs, and the highly muscular foot used in movement. The mantle, an extension of the body wall, secretes a shell in some groups. In most groups, the mouth has a long, toothed structure, called a radula, used in rasping food.

Chitons (Class Polyplacophora)

Chitons are ancient creatures that have evolved very little since they appeared thousands of years ago. Their flattened, oval-shaped body, large muscular foot, and mantle of overlapping plates, make these creatures specially adapted for adhering tightly to whatever substrate they are on. The radula, a kind of roughened tongue, is used to scrape algae from rocks for food.

Gastropods (Class Gastropoda)

This group contains nearly 80 percent of all living mollusks. Only a few members of this vast group are treated here, because a companion volume, *Familiar Seashells*, covers them exclusively. Gastropods have a spiral shell into which the creature can retract and hide. The limpet's shell is modified to protect a foot, which attaches firmly to substrates. Sea hares have a rudimentary shell within their mantle, while nudibranchs only have shells during their larval stage.

Octopi and Squid (Class Cephalopoda)

The most specialized of the mollusks, octopi and squid are among the most advanced of all invertebrates. They have a well-developed sensory system and brain, are capable of learning, and have excellent eyesight. The mantle encloses the entire visceral mass. The arms are equipped with suckers, and the mouth has a beak that is used in capturing and tearing apart food.

Arthropods (Phylum Arthropoda)	Between 80 and 90 percent of all named creatures on earth are arthropods, a group that includes the insects as well as the three classes described below. All have a rigid exoskeleton made up of chitin, and grow through a series of molts. There are three generalized body regions: head, thorax, and abdomen.
Horseshoe Crab (Class Merostomata)	Of five species worldwide, only one lives in American waters, along the Atlantic Coast. It has a spinelike tail, a carapace that covers the mouth and legs, and an abdomen that covers the gills and sexual organs.
Sea Spiders (Class Pycnogonida)	Despite their superficial resemblance to terrestrial spiders, these creatures are only remotely related to the arachnids. Some sea spiders have 12 or 14 legs. They are predators, feeding on the juices of animals such as sponges, bryozoans, and corals.
Shrimps, Lobsters, Crabs, Barnacles (Class Crustacea) 	This is a large and varied group, which includes more than 30,000 living species. All crustaceans are aquatic, and all have two pairs of antennae and three pairs of feeding appendages along with their varied numbers of walking or swimming appendages.

Echinoderms (Phylum Echinodermata)

The radial symmetry of echinoderms' bodies, which are arranged into five equal parts, is the most obvious characteristic in this family. Three types of fluids are contained in the various cavities of the body—blood, the main visceral body fluids, and a water-vascular system that provides a hydraulic system for the tube feet used in feeding, movement, and breathing. "Echinoderm" means "spiny skin," and refers to these creatures' spines or small warty bumps.

Sea Stars (Class Stelleroidea, Subclass Asteroidea)

Members of this unmistakable group have bodies shaped like stars or pentagons. Most species have five arms joining a central disk, although sun stars may have up to 14 arms. Paired rows of suckerlike tube feet lie in grooves on the underside of each arm; they are used in movement and for grasping prey.

Brittle Stars, Basket Stars (Class Stelleroidea, Subclass Ophiuroidea)

Daintier in appearance than sea stars, these creatures have arms that generally attach directly to the central disk and are sharply set off from one another. The arms of brittle stars are long, slender, and unbranching, but those of basket stars are heavily branched.

Sea Urchins, Sand Dollars (Class Echinoidea)

Sea urchins are nearly spherical, while sand dollars may be flattened. The endoskeleton is made up of rigid, closely fitted plates, and the body is usually covered with sharp, movable spines. The gnawing mouth structure is known as "Aristotle's lantern." Tube feet tipped with suckers occur around the body.

Sea Cucumbers (Class Holothuroidea)

The radially symmetrical body of Sea Cucumbers is elongated and lies on its side. The soft body wall is thin to leathery. The body is supported by the endoskeleton, which is made up of microscopic spines embedded in the body wall. Sea cucumbers have no external spines or arms. Their mouths are usually surrounded by tentacles, used in feeding. Their vascular system is made up of body fluids, rather than the sea water found in the other groups of echinoderms.

Bryozoans (Phylum Bryozoa)

With more than 4,000 living species found today, Bryozoans occur all over the world in a broad array of environmental conditions. Most are colonial and sedentary. They secrete protective cases around themselves, which generally fuse to others in the colony. The colonies are almost always attached to rocks, vegetation, or the bodies of other animals.

Chordates (Phylum Chordata)

Chordate animals are named for the presence of a notochord, a stiffened rod composed of cells wrapped in a firm sheath, which provides structure but allows flexibility. Instead of stretching, the notochord allows the chordate body to bend only from side to side. Other than the Urochordates listed below and lancelets (not described in this book), all chordates are vertebrates.

Tunicates, Salps (Phylum Chordata, Subphylum Urochordata)

The notochord is only found in the larval, free-swimming stage of these creatures, and the adults bear no resemblance at all to other chordate creatures. Salps are transparent, barrel-shaped planktonic creatures that use their incurrent and excurrent siphons to pull water through their bodies to move. The tunicates, or sea squirts, are usually attached to sedentary objects, and may be either solitary or colonial. They use ciliated cells to move water through incurrent siphons into the central body cavity and out through excurrent siphons.

Glossary

Aristotle's lantern
The chewing mechanism of a sea urchin, consisting of 5 teeth operated by a complex system of levers and muscles.

Bioluminescence
Light produced by a living organism through a biochemical reaction.

Budding
A mode of asexual reproduction in which an outgrowth of an organism develops and forms a new individual.

Carapace
That part of the exoskeleton of a horseshoe crab or higher crustacean extending over the head and thorax, but not the abdomen.

Cilium
A microscopic, hairlike projection on the free border of epithelial cells that beats with others in coordinated waves (pl. cilia).

Comb plate
A comblike membrane of fused cilia in comb jellies (Ctenophora), used in movement.

Detritus
Particles worn off a solid body.

Exoskeleton
The rigid outer covering of an arthropod.

Flagellum
A whiplike appendage of a cell, used in locomotion or in creating a current (pl. flagella).

Hermaphroditic
Having the organs of both sexes in one individual.

Mantle
A sheet of tissue that lines and secretes the shell of a mollusk, or covers the outside of a shell-less mollusk, and encloses the mantle cavity.

Margin
The edge of the shell of a limpet or the edges of a bivalve.

Medusa
One of the body forms of a cnidarian, cup-shaped or bowl-shaped with a mouth on a stalk on the underside, and capable of swimming by rhythmic contractions.

Mesoglea
The jellylike layer between the epidermis and gastrodermis in a cnidarian.

Notochord
A cartilaginous band forming a primitive spinal column.

Parapodium
One of the paired appendages on the segments of a polychaete annelid (pl. parapodia).

Phylum (pl. phyla)
A major division of the Animal Kingdom, in which all members share fundamental characteristics such as general body plan, segmentation, and symmetry. Phyla are further divided into classes.

ncer
term used to designate the
perlike appendage of
staceans; the chela.

ncher
e nipperlike appendage of
tain bryozoans or echinoderms
ose function is to keep the
rface free of other settling
ganisms; also called an
icularium in the bryozoans, and
edicellaria in the echinoderms;
mouthpart in sea spiders.

ankton
collective term for all organisms
ing suspended in water, either
able to swim or swimming so
ebly as to be at the mercy of
ater currents.

lyp
e of the body forms of a
idarian, usually cylindrical, with
mouth surrounded by tentacles
one end and with the other end
tached.

Proboscis
An extensible or permanently
extended structure on the head,
commonly associated with the
mouth of an animal, used in
feeding or sensing food or other
chemical substances.

Radial symmetry
A body plan in which repeated
body parts are arranged around a
central point, as in a wheel.

Radula
The flexible, rasplike "tongue" of a
mollusk.

Segment
One of the serially repeated
divisions of the body of an annelid
or arthropod.

Siphon
An opening, frequently tubular,
through which an animal takes in
or expels water; a siphon carrying
water in is called an incurrent
siphon and a siphon carrying
water out is called an excurrent
siphon. Found in mollusks and
tunicates, among others.

Spicule
A small structure, often needlelike
or dartlike, supporting the tissues
of various sponges, soft corals, and
compound tunicates.

Substrate
The surface on which an organism
lives.

Test
The skeleton of an echinoid
echinoderm, consisting of rows of
fused plates.

Tube foot
One of the numerous small
appendages of an echinoderm,
hydraulically operated and used in
feeding or locomotion, or as a
sense organ; often tipped with a
suction disk.

Valve
One of the separate parts of a
mollusk or brachiopod shell.

Visceral mass
That part of the molluscan body
containing the visceral organs.

Index

Numbers in italics refer to seashore creatures mentioned as similar species.

A

Acanthodoris pilosa, 88
Acropora cervicornis, 52
Aeolidia papillosa, 92
Anemone, Frilled, 46
Anemone, Ghost, 50
Anemone, Striped, 48
Aplysia californica, 90
Aplysia dactylomela, *90*
Asterias vulgaris, 146
Aurelia aurita, 36

B

Balanus nubilis, 102
Barnacle, Common Goose, 100
Barnacle, Giant Acorn, 102
Basket Star, Northern, 148
Beroe cucumis, *62*
Bolinopsis infundibulum, *164*
Brittle Star, Daisy, *150*
Bryozoan, California Spiral-tufted, *164*
Bryozoan, Spiral-tufted, *164*
Bugula californica, *164*
Bugula turrita, 164

C

Callinectes sapidus, 126
Campanularia spp., 28
Cancer magister, *128*
Cancer productus, 128
Chiton, Lined, 174
Chrysaora melanaster, *32*
Chrysaora quinquecirrha, 32
Cistenides brevicoma, *77*
Ciona intestinalis, 166
Cliona celata, 24
Comb Jelly, Beroë's, *62*
Comb Jelly, Leidy's, 62
Coral, Clubbed Finger, 56
Coral, Fire, 50
Coral, Labyrinthine Brain, 58
Coral, Red Soft, 40
Coral, Staghorn, 52
Crab, Arrow, 140
Crab, Blue, 126
Crab, Common Spider, 138
Crab, Ghost, 134
Crab, Horseshoe, 106
Crab, Long-clawed Hermit, 122
Crab, Pacific Mole, 124
Crab, Purple Marsh, 132
Crab, Purple Shore, 130
Crab, Red, 128
Crossaster papposus, 142
Cucumaria frondosa, *160*
Cucumaria miniata, 160
Cyanea capillata, 34

D

Dendraster excentricus, *158*
Dendronotus frondosus, 86
Diadema antillarum, 154
Diadumene leucolena, 50
Diploria labyrinthiformes, 58
Doliolid, Common, *172*
Doliolum nationalis, *172*
Doris, Hairy, 88

E

Echinarachnius parma, 158
Emerita analoga, 124
Eucidaris tribuloides, 156
Eudistylia polymorpha, 82
Eurythoe complanata, 74

F

Feather Duster, Giant, 82
Flatworm, Tapered, 66

tworm, Zebra, 64
a, California Beach, 108

semia rubiformis, 40
gonocephalus arcticus, 148

liclona oculata, 18
liclona permollis, 20
liclystus salpinx, 38
liplanella luciae, 48
lyocynthia pyriformis, 170
migrapsus oregonensis, 130
migrapsus nudus, 130
marus americanus, 116
droid, Feathered, 26
droid, Wine-glass, 28

lyfish, Moon, 36
lyfish, Trumpet Stalked, 38

oas anatifera, 100
pidonotus squamatus, 70
inia emarginata, 138
npet, Giant Keyhole, 176
nulus polyphemus, 106

Lineus, Red, 68
Lineus ruber, 68
Lion's Mane, 34
Lobster, California Rock, 120
Lobster, Northern, 116
Lobster, Ridged Slipper, 118
Loligo opalescens, 94
Loligo pealei, 94
Lysmata wurdemanni, 114

M

Man-of-war, Portuguese, 30
Megathura crenulata, 176
Metridium senile, 46
Microciona prolifera, 22
Millepora alcicornis, 50
Mnemiopsis leidyi, 62

N

Nereis virens, 72
Notoplana acticola, 66
Nudibranch, Maned, 92

O

Octopus, Common Atlantic, 96
Octopus dofleini, 96
Octopus, Giant Pacific, 96
Octopus vulgaris, 96
Ocypode quadrata, 134

Ophiopholis aculeata, 150
Orchestoidea californiana, 108

P

Pachygrapsus crassipes, 130
Pachygrapsus transversus, 130
Pagurus granosimanus, 122
Pagurus longicarpus, 122
Pandalus borealis, 110
Pandalus danae, 110
Panulirus orgas, 120
Panulirus interruptus, 120
Patiria miniata, 144
Pectinaria californiensis, 76
Pectinaria gouldii, 76
Penaeus aztecus, 112
Penaeus duorarum, 112
Penaeus setiferus, 112
Pennaria tiarella, 26
Phoxichilidium femoratum, 98
Phyllodoce spp., 80
Physalia physalis, 30
Pleurobrachia bachei, 60
Pleurobrachia pileus, 60
Polycirrus eximius, 78
Porites porites, 56
Ptilosarcus gurneyi, 44

S

Salp, Common, 172
Salp, Horned, *172*
Salpa fusiformis, 172
Sand Dollar, Common, 158
Sand Fiddler, 136
Sclerodactyla briareus, 162
Scyllarides nodifer, 118
Sea Cucumber, Hairy, 162
Sea Cucumber, Red, 160
Sea Gooseberry, 60
Sea Hare, California, 90
Sea Nettle, 32
Sea Peach, 170
Sea Pen, Gurney's, 44
Sea Slug, Bushy-backed, 86
Sea Spider, Clawed, 98
Sea Star, Northern, 146
Sea Urchin, Green, 152
Sea Urchin, Long-spined, 154
Sea Vase, 166
Sesarma cinereum, *132*
Sesarma reticulatum, 132
Shrimp, Common Mantis, 104
Shrimp, Coon-stripe, 110
Shrimp, Pink, 112
Shrimp, Red-lined Cleaning, 114
Spirobranchus giganteus, 84
Spirobranchus spinosus, *84*

Sponge, Boring, 24
Sponge, Finger, 18
Sponge, Purple, 20
Sponge, Red Beard, 22
Squid, Atlantic Long-fin, 94
Squilla empusa, 104
Star, Bat, 144
Sternorhynchus seticornis, 140
Strongylocentrotus droebachiensis, 152
Strongylocentrotus purpuratus, 152
Styela montereyensis, 168
Styela plicata, *168*
Stylochus zebra, 64
Sun Star, Spiny, 142

T

Talorchestia megalophthalma, *108*
Thalia democratica, *172*
Tonicella lineata, 174
Tunicate, Monterey Stalked, 168
Tunicate, Striped, *168*

U

Uca crenulata, *136*
Uca pugilator, 136
Urchin, Slate-pencil, 156

W

Worm, Clam, 72
Worm, Ice Cream Cone, 76
Worm, Orange Fire, 74
Worm, Red Terrebellid, 78
Worm, Spiral-gilled Tube, 84
Worm, Twelve-scaled, 70
Worm, Leafy Paddle, 80

▶tographers
▶iam H. Amos (65, 89, 109, 113,)
▶rles Arneson (67, 99, 105)
▶. Degginger (73, 91, 127)

▶th Images
▶id Denning (37)

▶ Foott (169)
▶iel W. Gotshall (103, 161, 175,)

▶rotell (19, 25, 43, 57, 59, 115, ▶

▶ Myers (97)

▶ional Audubon Society
▶lection/Photo Researchers, Inc.
▶ert Dunne (71, 151, 159),
▶ion H. Levy (31), Fred
▶onnaughey (55), Tom McHugh
▶ 111, 121, 125, 129), Tom
▶Hugh/Steinhart Aquarium (83),
▶rew J. Martinez (117), Stephen
▶arker (131), S. Richards (145),
▶rge Whiteley (137)

▶.Pratt (23, 27, 29, 33, 39, 51,
▶ 63, 69, 77, 79, 81, 87, 95, 107,
▶ 139, 147, 149, 155, 163, 165,
▶, 171, 173)

Valan Photos
Paul L. Janosi (47, 53, 75, 85, 93,
141, 157), Stephen J. Krasemann
(135, 153), R. La Salle (21, 41, 49,
143), J.R. Page (101), Alan
Wilkinson (35)

Illustrators
Silhouettes by Paul Singer
Drawings by Dolores R.
Santoliquido

Chanticleer Press
Publisher: Andrew Stewart
Senior Editor: Ann Whitman
Editor: Carol M. Healy
Project Editor: Ann ffolliott
Editorial Assistant: Kate Jacobs
Production: Kathy Rosenbloom,
Karyn Slutsky
Project Design: Paul Zakris
Photo Library: Tim Allan

Natural Science Consultant: John
Farrand, Jr.
Series Design: Massimo Vignelli

The Audubon Society

The NATIONAL AUDUBON SOCIETY, incorporated in 1905, is one of the oldest and largest conservation organizations in the world. Named after American wildlife artist and naturalist, John James Audubon, the Society has nearly 600,000 members in 500 chapters, nine regional and five state offices, as well as a government affairs center in Washington, D.C. Its headquarters are in New York City.

The Society works on behalf of our natural heritage through scientific research, environmental education, and conservation action. It maintains a network of almost 90 wildlife sanctuaries nationwide, conducts ecology camps for adults, and youth programs for schoolchildren. The Society publishes the leading conservation and nature magazine, *Audubon;* an ornithological journal, *American Birds;* and World of Audubon Television Specials, newsletters, video cassettes and interactive discs, and other educational materials.

For further information regarding membership in the Society, write to the NATIONAL AUDUBON SOCIETY, 950 Third Avenue, New York, N.Y. 10022.